A wallflower
In the wild

KAUSAR KAASHIFA

ILLUSTARATED BY
ZUWAIRIYA

For my heart

At last, I have unburdened you

Of the things you could not say

Dear reader,

As you embark on this poetic journey, you might find
pieces of your own story within these pages. I hope you
find comfort and connection in these verses. You may
experience a range of emotions while reading this book,
and I want you to know that it's okay to feel certain things
or even everything at once. But remember that you're not
alone.

Love,

Kausar

ACKNOWLEDGMENTS

I would like to extend my heartfelt gratitude to everyone who has helped me and supported me on this journey.

To my amazing husband, thank you for walking beside me in every chapter of my life and giving me the love and support through every step I take. Your love has always been an anchor holding me strong through tough times.

To my family- my mother and siblings, thank you for your endless support. Mom, you have shaped me, supported me, guided me through everything, and taught me valuable lessons, because of you I am this person now. To my siblings, your understanding and presence has always been a source of comfort and happiness through my tough times and for that I owe you everything.

To my incredible friends, your laughter, wisdom and companionship have always been my source of joy and strength. Thank you for the endless conversations, the shared dreams and lifting me up when I needed. Near or far, your love has always been a light in my life.

To the keeper of my stories, thank you for your silent strength. And to my close friend, who has helped me with this book and whose talent and creativity has bought this book to life through illustrations. Thank you for sharing this with me.

Lastly, to you my dearest readers, this book is a piece of my heart and I thank you for holding it and letting it speak to your heart. I'm honored to share this journey with you.

About the Author

Kausar Kaashifa, author of Crestfallen Nights and A Wallflower in the wild, writes poetry that resonates with raw emotion, capturing the delicate balance of love, loss, womanhood and healing. Kausar is inspired by the everyday moments that reveal life's most profound truths. As a wife and a mother, she writes to offer solace and strength encouraging others to embrace their own stories of resilience. Her poetry serves as a reminder that even in the darkest of times, hope and healing are possible.

You can discover more of her work and connect with her @kausarpoetry

CONTENTS

INTRODUCTION

In these pages you'll find the pieces of me that were loved, that were torn down, the struggles of being born a woman and the healing and acceptance that happened eventually. The inspiration for this collection is mostly from my personal experience and a little bit of fiction.

There are some things I wish I could say to people but for some reason I could never open up my mouth. I always bottle up my emotions and sometimes I wish I could let them all out but I never could. But by writing this book I could finally express my emotions and thoughts. Afterall I actually have a way to let them out.

When people like me fall in love, we express them through writing letters, sending them a big paragraph of text or perhaps even writing about it in a diary. But in my case, I've written a chapter about the things that they did to make me happy and the littlest things they notice when I thought no one would notice.

I think there are a lot of individuals out there who are exactly like me unable to express their thoughts and emotions openly, fearing that someone who don't even know us that well would say something that might break our hearts. Similarly In the chapter hurt, you'll discover the various heartbreaking things people did and the emotional struggles I faced with those I once loved.

Womanhood is a profound journey marked by vulnerability, strength, fragility and tenderness where life unfolds the unique challenges and triumphs as she goes through. In the chapter womanhood you'll discover the silent battles she fights, the complexities, the gender discrimination, the love she shows her children and the life of a mother in a typical Indian household.

Finally, you'll see how everything has affected me, teaching me to love, face, and embrace womanhood and how healing gradually unfolds through the process of letting go.

These verses are raw and honest which I hope brings you a comfort on your own untold stories.

. . .

LOVE

• • •

Handwritten notes,
With verses from love quotes,
Passed under wooden desks
Where hands gently touched,
Words exchanged in silent chants,
A sudden flinch,
A subtle smile.

She quietly read and folded the paper,
Taking it home to store with the others.
From the smallest note
To the longest letter,
She saved them all.

She read them over and over,
And each time, they made her smile,
Reminding her of the love
That passed quietly
Under the wooden desk.

~little things in love

I was on the verge of being swallowed
By the demons inside my head.
I had fallen to the ground,
Broken and crying.
But then I saw you.
You came like the prince charming
I had read about in fairytales.
You fought the deadly demons
And saved me, just like a fairytale prince.
Now, you love me the way a prince loves—
With strength, grace, and kindness.
And now I believe,
This is our happily ever after.

In the middle of the night,
With starlight
And streetlights,
We drove past
The misty lake,
With wind in my hair
And you by my side.
Felt like living inside
A romance novel.

Sunrises on my terrace,
Sunsets by the beaches
And sunflowers in my garden
Remind me of you!

From the moment our eyes met,
I sensed a tangled invisible string
Attached to our intertwined hearts.
I was struggling to listen to your heartbeat
From a distance, clouded by doubts,
But you gently untangled the string
And pulled me closer to listen
To a rhythmic pulse meant only for me.

One sunny day,
As spring began,
The lakes were glistening,
Flowers blooming beautifully
Birds swinging and singing,
And we sat below the cherry blossoms,
Holding hands, and watching our children play.

There are certain people in my life
Who said, "I'll be there" and actually did.
Those guys made me laugh
Until I cried and my tummy ached.
When I am with them,
I never felt the need to hide my heart.
When I struggled to find the real version of me
I realized it was with them I was being me.
We would sing songs with deep voices
And we would dance like there was no tomorrow.
Sometimes, we feel motivated to lose weight,
And sometimes we just order junk and eat.
But we would always stick together,
Make sure everyone was okay,
And everyone had their food regularly.
No matter how busy we were,
At the end of the day, we would sit in a circle
And talk about the day we had.
People who do those things are family.
And they are my family. They are home.

Just a single look
My hands trembled,
My body turned flaming heat,
My palms dripping of sweat,
My cheeks turned pale pink,
My mouth ran out of words.

~meeting for the first time

You're like the flower,
Gentle and rare,
Oh, my lover, my heart
Blooms when you're near.

I'm like the bee,
Buzzing in circles around you
Though at times I sting,
You're the nectar I need,

You're sweet and tender,
Your touch a delicate feather
And your scent, I'd surrender,
You and I always belong together.

I love your brown eyes
Do you know why?
When the sun hits them
They look like a pool of honey
Oh, would you take a look at me?
I could drown in them forever
How could I take my eyes off you?
Oh no, I am drowning.

It's not the situation
That made us fall in love.
It was destiny.
We were destined to be together
Even before
The sun,
The moon,
The stars,
And the universe was created.
We were written into each other's stories
And were meant to be intertwined for a
lifetime.

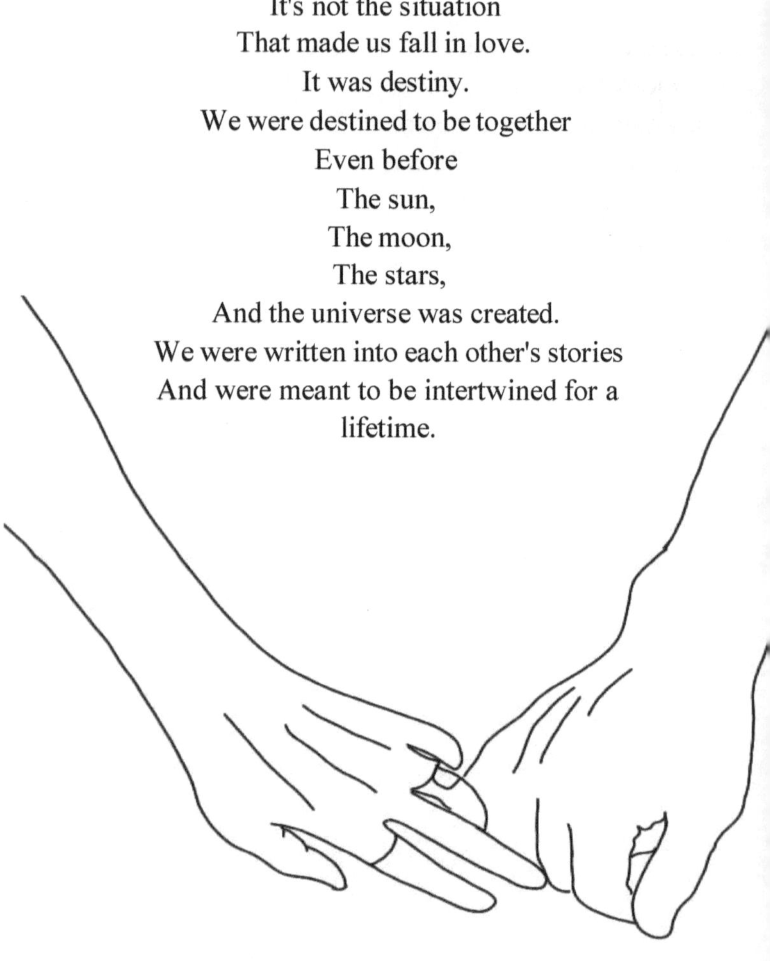

I remember the time
When we first started talking
Which lasted till 3 a.m.

I remember the time
When we used to have long video chats
And the way we'd blush seeing each other.

I remember the time
When we had late-night dates
And night walk by the lakes.

I remember the time
When we danced with the stars
To the song "A thousand years."

I remember the time
When we looked into each other's eyes
And realized we were in love.

I recall them every time,
Every time we fight.
That way, I'll remember how much I love you,
How many memories we made,
And how much it hurts me not to be with you.
No matter how hard our lives get
No matter how hard this relationship gets,
I will never give up on us.

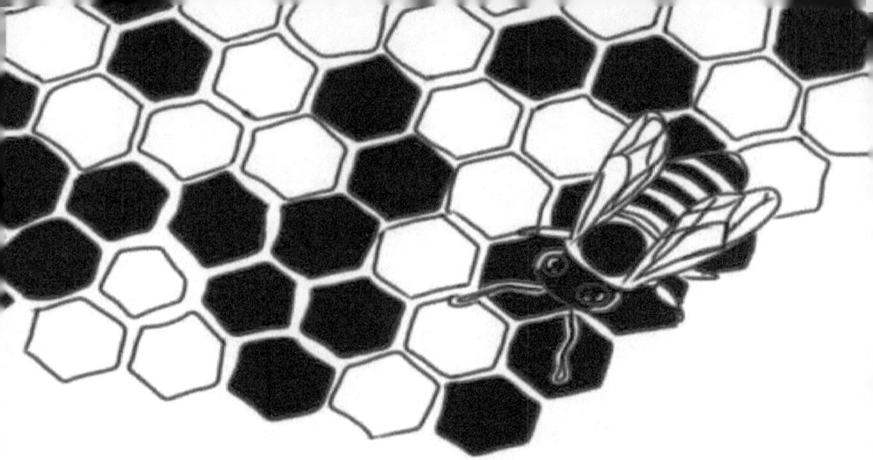

Bees always buzz around your mind,
Learn to live with peace.
Let not Your sweet brown eyes
Drip unsweetened honey.
If not, the bears will snatch your hive
And eat you alive.
But do not fear them,
For I would always protect you
From those life-threatening predators.

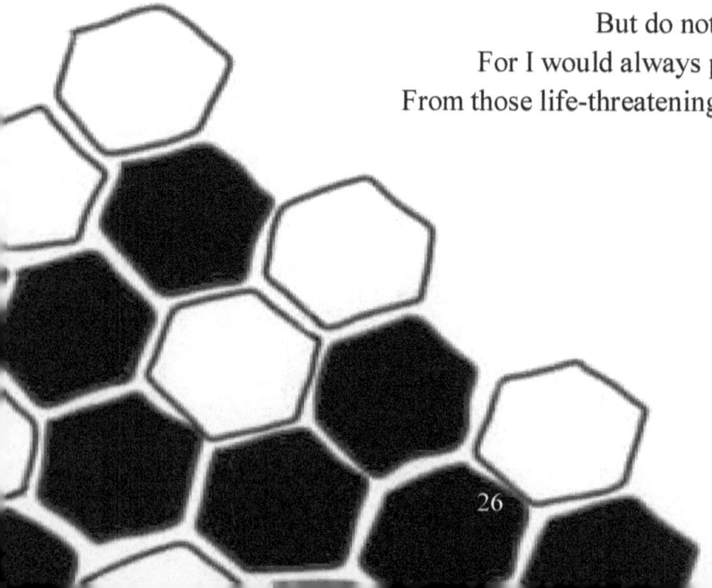

When I see you,
My blood rush and I blush,
O' you great magician,
Could you predict the day
You would be mine?

It's almost twilight,
Time for our date night.
I can smell your Christian Dior
Just before you knock at my door.
You arrive in a black suit
With a bouquet in hand,
And held my hand with grace.
A kiss, soft as feather,
And offer the flowers so elegantly.

Under moonlight, with candlelight,
We dine, we laugh, we talk slow.
Then you rise turning on the music,
A perfect melody fills the room.
You ask for my hand, we start to dance,
I hold your strong, veiny hands.
You pull me close,
A perfect rhythm,
With perfect moves.

As the song slowly fades
You hold my face,
And kiss, a kiss so tender,
And softly whisper,
 "I love you."

He protects me like a knight,
Guarding me, never out of sight.
He's younger than me
But with wisdom beyond his years.
He's always by my side, standing strong
And correcting me when I'm wrong.
He has always loved me,
And cared for me like a father.
To him, I owe every success,
For his love is my greatest gift.

~ my little brother

We strolled along the pavement
The streets were quiet and still.
You took my hand,
Pulled me into the street.
We danced to the rhythm
Of our heartbeat.
Our eyes met
Hearts in perfect sync.
A first drop of rain kissed my lips,
I looked at the sky
Grey clouds gathered,
And it was about to rain.
You leaned in and kissed
Where the first rain drop fell.
We looked each other with love in our hearts
And when the rain started to pour,
You held my me tight,
While I wrapped my arms
around yours,
And my head resting gently
on your shoulder.
We walked slowly living the
moment.
It was an enchanting night,
And a beautiful dream.

Sometimes I do lie,
Not because I want to,
But because I fear
You might get hurt.
I love you so much,
And I would never
Do anything to hurt you.

This love is exciting
When we still feel butterflies.
This love is beautiful
In the little glances we share.
This love is madness
When we fight or misunderstand.
This love is magical
When we bring each other's fantasies to life.
This love is everlasting
When we promise an eternity.
This love is true
When everything fades but us.

This love is you,
Only you,
And it will always be you.

I Love your scars,
Even the ones that are
Hiding inside your beard.

I was in love with
The brightest star.
When it left me,
I was searching for
The star my whole life.
But then I forgot
About the moon,
Who was with me
The whole time.

It was a dreary and cruel December
When people were turning nefarious
And losing everything in the labyrinth,
It made me fear my own silhouette.
Nevertheless, you held my hand
And opened the gates of neverland.
Watching a picturesque view beside you
And watching the flames of fire
Turn into crimson embers
Was all my euphoric heart ever wanted.

You know me
More than I know myself.
You know what I'm thinking,
When I sit silently in a corner,
And the words I'm about to say
When I can't find the right ones.

You know what I love and hate,
You catch my lies
Even when I try to hide them.
You know all my stories
The unheard friendships,
The love,
The heartbreak,
The family.

You remember everything I said,
And everything I did.
You even remember that girl's name
That I mentioned only once,
And the dress I wore
On that Saturday night in 2016.
I don't know how you do it,
But I adore it.
Having someone
Who listens,
Who looks out for me,
And remembers every little piece of me.
You are my human diary,
The keeper of my stories,
The one who knows me better than anyone.
In you, I find not just a friend—
But the home where my heart rests.

You're the sun, I'm your rays,
You're the moon, I'm your light,
You're the stars that I love at night.
Together we'll make the world shine bright.

It's almost January,
The night of New Year's Eve.
Watching the snowfall,
Standing with you
On the balcony,
Wrapped in cozy sheets.
As the clock strikes twelve
And fireworks begin,
We start to kiss—
Oh, what a wonderful way
To begin the year.

While flipping through old photo albums,
I found a picture of us—
You with your bowl cut,
Me with my bob cut.
We stood side by side,
I wore a pink dress,
You in a blue shirt
and frameless glasses.

Who could have known, back then,
That I would marry you?
Years later we returned to the same spot,
Took another picture
Me in a dress so similar,
You, still in blue, but now with framed glasses.
Smiling for the camera,
I'm flooded with déjà vu,
And I feel that time has brought us
Back to where we began.

After all this time,
You still give me butterflies.
Even your obvious lies
Makes me laugh.
But I do adore them.

Dark is not scary,
It's neither eerie,
But rather merry,
When you are near me.

Not everyone likes
Expensive gifts.
People like me cherish
Handwritten letters.

I love you
Very truly,
Very deeply,
And passionately.
But I've never shown it
In an expressive way.
You were around me all the time
So, I thought you'd never leave me alone.
But when you left for a week's work
And never returned for a month,
It made me think, I should've shown you
How much I loved you
When you were around me
Very truly,
Very deeply,
And passionately.

I'm happy to see the relationship
You have with our daughter.
It's nothing like my dad and me.
When I see the love between you two
I cannot control my smile and my tears.
The way you handle our daughter
The way you bond over little things,
The way you make her feel happy,
The way you do silly faces,
Just to see the smile on her face.
I could just say that,
She has got the best father ever.
I see my whole world in front of me.
It's so magical, and when I see you,
I see a golden garden,
Filled with ruby roses
And you in the middle playing with her
While I watch my heart and soul together
Making my life content forever.

The Lashes

I gave him a chocolate hidden inside a book. He smiled and looked at me. He took the chocolate and returned the book the next day. He also told me to have a look at his watch. I didn't know what he was trying to say, but he insisted I take a closer look. When I did, I was overwhelmed. My eyes were filled with tears as I realized what he had done. The book I had given him had my fallen eyelash which he preserved inside his watch. Thinking back, it makes me happy that someone has loved me with such devotion, but also makes me sad knowing that I may never be loved like that again.

Never have I ever thought I would love you
Although fate works in mysterious ways.
Vividly I remember the first time we met
Everything began to make sense right then.
Every cell within me was ecstatic.
Thereafter, you became my only happiness
Having to love and to be loved by you was my dream.

All the time,
I stand by the window,
Thinking of you,
Watching the starlight and the moon.
But when the wind whispers through,
I feel you by my side.

We have talked about everything
Our past stories,
Our future fantasies,
And the things in between.
Now, with no more topics to discuss
We sit in quiet,
Staring into each other's eyes.

And then I realized,
Our silence and our eyes
Could speak a million beautiful words
Without a sound,
Without a blink,
We understand each other.
By diving deep
Into each other's eyes.

I had a lot of friends
They were around me all the time.
They'd look everyone with their judgy eyes,
Obviously, I do know when they lie.
They'd boast more about themselves,
I would just listen without interrupting.
I'd try to fit in and laugh at their jokes,
If they seem a little sad, I'd console them.
I'd try to understand their complicated talks
Even if I don't understand, I would just nod along.
I never wanted to seem dumb
In front of all my brilliant friends.

They think they know me very well,
But They only know me as a quiet
And a soft-spoken girl.
Everything has changed now,
Everybody has left me.
I longed for someone who'd
Know me even if I didn't talk much.
I needed someone to share my thoughts,
I needed a shoulder to cry on.

There was complete darkness.
And then you stepped in,
Bringing your sunshine

In my darkened room
And making it better and brighter.
I've found someone who'd listen,
Who'd write me letters and poems,
Who'd listen to my rambling,
And where I could act like a total nut crack,
Knowing that there'd be no judgment,
Knowing that someone always has my back.

I've found a safe place,
 I've been searching this for my whole life
For a love so pure,
For a love so special.
Now that I've found you,
I would always protect you with my life,
I would always stay by your side,
And I would always love you with my heart.

Friends can turn into families,

But families can never turn into friends.

When I'm about to turn away and leave,
I want you to hold my hand,
Look me in the eye and say,
"Don't leave me, honey–
I love you!"

You love tulips
I love roses.
You love sunrise
I love sunsets.
You love movies
I love books.
You love songs
I love poems.
You love me,
And
I love you.

When I was in the process of healing
I saw you, and just got the feeling
That you might be the one
The perfect guy from the ton.
And I was right,
From the first sight.

You healed me and stood by me
Helping me face each fear,
Wiping away all my tears.
I knew you were the one,
The one who was written for me.

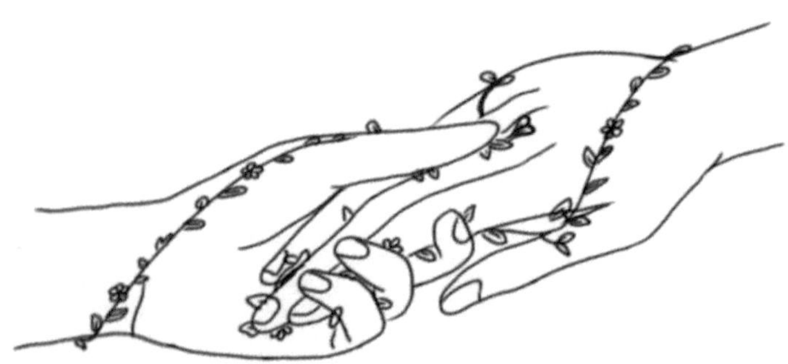

Dearest Christopher

Every sunrise and sunset must be magical
Seeing from the ship you're sailing.
Hearing the winds howling like a wolf,
Watching the moon waxing and waning,
Trying to count the endless stars
Must be breathtaking and magnificent.
You're somewhere in the middle of the sea,
Traveling and exploring new places and people.
Sometimes you might wonder about life,
Sometimes you might be stuck in a dilemma,
Sometimes you might just want to disappear.
Just remember you have someone
Whom you can count on,
And who'll always be there for you.
I guess it's time for you
To put down your compass and map
And return to the land as soon as possible.
Your loved ones are longing
and waiting for your return by the docks.

~waiting for a friend

I would never say that you were an accident
I never thought you'd become my heart resident.
I never expected you would stay this long,
I never assumed you'd be the same all along.
I want what we have to last forever
I want us to grow old, holding hands,
Not letting go until we reach,
The gates of paradise.

HURT

When the cold winds howled,
They took as many leaves as they could,
Leaving the tree bare and alone.
Just like the wind, you took from me
All the wonderful things I used to be,
Leaving me lost, utterly alone.

I shouldn't have smiled
The first time we met.
I shouldn't have waved back
The first time you said hello.
I shouldn't have said "I love you"
When we realized we were in love.
I should've stopped you
The first time we kissed.
I should've stopped you
At the very beginning.
I shouldn't have dragged you
Into the mess I already had.
I'm sorry I'm miserable.
It's my fault too.
I agree-it's my fault too.

~guilty

Maybe in a parallel universe
I hope you'll be a better father

I still bleed all the way along,
Trying to cure my inner child.
I'm stuck in a world where I do not belong,
Still stumbling towards the next part.

I have trust issues after escaping toxicity.
I still fight with my old demons,
Barely able to handle the new ones.
I still see darkness
And can no longer keep my waves calm.

I left every place that felt too comfortable.
I left every soul who would die for me.
I feared their arrival and became vulnerable.
But now I'm relieved when they left for good
Yet they live in my head like dancing demons.

Anxiety, fear, shivers, doubts,
Took over their place.
So, I sit beneath the willow tree
Wondering if I could ever recover from them.

I have a lot of things going on in my mind.
I wish I could tell them,
But I don't want to destroy your peace of mind.
So, I'll smile conceal my heart
And tell you the sweetest lies.
Somethings are better that way.

You said you'd listen to me
On a sad, long day,
But it always ends with you—

~The friend who talks more about themselves

Whenever I think about you
There is an unfinished poem

Little by little,
I'm forgetting all
The memories of my childhood-
The people, the laughter and the places.
Once they were vivid, but now
They are fading away.

Maybe one day,
The smile and face of yours
Will be blurred and faded,
And the echoing voice in my mind
Will be distant and long gone.
And perhaps I'll forget you too.

I am always the quiet girl,
The one who would never talk,
The one who would never say no,
The one who'd always agrees to everything.
When I couldn't handle it anymore,
They labeled me as
The girl who talks back,
The girl who is so stubborn,
The girl who couldn't handle her anger,
The girl who is so selfish.
After hearing all those awful things
I had to handle that chaos,
So, I went back to being the same girl.
Who became even more
Quieter
And
Quieter.

I hate it whenever you'd say,
"I know what you're thinking right now"
Fearing you every time,
I'd say, " You always get me right"
But there's not even a single time
You were right.

I tried so much to make you stay,
I pleaded you not to leave me this way.
But you've already decided to leave
On the beautiful night of New Year's Eve,
Without even giving me a sweet last kiss.
You packed, so I assume you weren't going to miss.
So, stop telling me those hoax vows.
I hope you realize you were someone's true love.

Why am I always
A people's pleaser?
When they're always disguised
As my heart's reaper.

Even if you don't miss me,
I still miss you.
Even if you don't think about me,
I still think about you.
Even if you don't love me,
I still love you.

When I'm angry about something,
I do not break anything kept inside the room.
I don't scream at the top of my lungs.
I don't swear, spilling out all the mean words.
I become silent and cry till my head headaches
Then I wash my face and come out of the room,
Smiling at everyone like nothing happened.

My mother had been held captive for 15 years,
Hiding and suppressing all her tears and fears.
She was trying to save the lives of her children
From the terrible sadistic beasts who live there.
She's been tortured mercilessly but still stayed,
Hoping her children would be safe and sound.
But when she realized
her children would be their next prey,
She took off and saved them-
And herself-from their wrath.
It took a while for my mother to realize,
But it's not too late-you could save yourself
From the beasts living inside your home too.

~ get away from toxic relationships

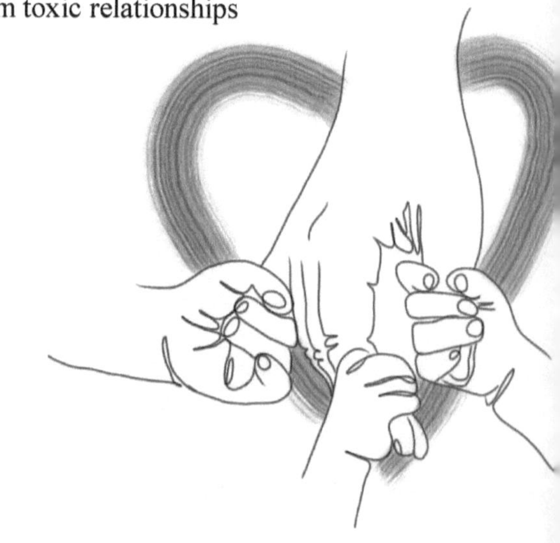

If you're going to break my heart this way,
You should've given me a slight inkling.
I wouldn't have wasted my ink and paper on you.
I would've shielded my heart in iron armor-
Even though it would break into a million pieces,
At least It would've protected my woeful heart.

After all these years
When I think about you
I still shed a few tears.

I hope you'll understand
The way you treated my mother
And realize that you've made a mistake

Buildings and bridges are being torn down,
Bombed town after town,
Making children orphans,
And killing the unborn in their mother's womb.
Babies are beheaded,
Women are brutally raped,
Men are being tortured,
The surviving people are struggling to live,
Not knowing whether they'll live tomorrow,
Or die while they are sleeping in fear.
And the whole country is being burned alive.
And you're playing the victim card,
With the most ignorant and shallow people behind you,
Who knows nothing about humanity,
 And boldly claiming what is not rightfully yours.

~ the war

Dear land,
I am just as mad as you are.
They're fighting
A useless war on you,c
Just to be swallowed by you.

You told me you were an archer—
I thought we'd be like the bow and arrow,
Bound together, aiming as one.
But who would've thought
You'd aim straight for my heart?

I had a place called home
I loved my room and my bed.
I'd roam around and I'd sleep all day,
With no sadness and no one to comment.

But seeing all the drama that happened
I desperately wanted to leave,
Thinking I do not belong there.
One fine day, I happened to leave,
And I reached a place where
I thought it was going to be my new home.

Turns out, I do not belong there either.
Even if they didn't say anything,
It is difficult for me to co-exist,
Knowing they all hate me.
I hesitate to do every little thing.

Now, when I try to go back
To the one place I called home,
I could never really go,
Or could stay long enough.
The place I thought I'd feel at home
never enjoyed my company,
And never really felt like home.

Now, where will I go
If I don't have a place to call
My home?

I am still haunted by the hunters,
Who gave me wounds and made me bleed,
Made every scar dive down deep.
I pleaded them not to go on a killing spree,
So, they plotted to smother their daughter.
I tirelessly ran, not knowing where it leads,
I did escape their plots and wrath,
But I trapped all their demonic acts in my head.
Now it's just a dream, but I still can't fall asleep.

If he doesn't
Hold your hand,
Take you out on dates,
Compliment your dress,
Hear out your dreams,
He may not be the one.

You told me to wait for four years,
And I did.
You told me to wait for two more years,
And I did.
Now you come and tell me
That this will never work.
Why did you make me believe
That you would come for me?
Why did you make me wait
When you could've ended it when it began?

Just like the contrails stay in the sky
Leave a mark and disappear,
 You loved me, hurt me, and then left me.

When everyone walked
Holding the hands of their father,
Laughing and talking
I used to walk behind him,
With my hands trembling,
With anxiety and nervousness.

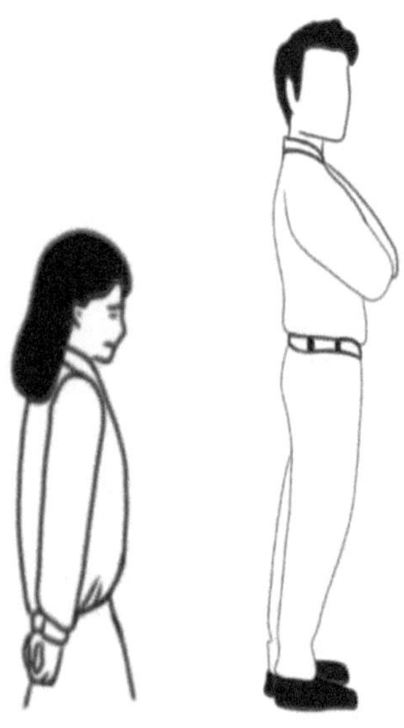

We met as strangers
Had a wonderful time,
Taking each other's sadness,
Turning them into beautiful moments,
Building a little castle of happiness,
And turning our friendship into love.
Just when I thought life was beautiful,
The little castle in our hearts
Had crashed and collapsed.
I guess it could never be fixed.
Everything went back to the way it was.
From unknown strangers
To known strangers.

I will never forget the things you stated,
It has been engraved in my heart.
I will never forget the drama you created,
With all those lies and fake crying.
When all I did was try to prove my point,
I know I didn't do anything wrong,
But you framed me as the wrongdoer,
That made my miserable mind think
I did something abysmal.
Your tears made me feel
Like I did something regrettable,
Even though I knew you were
Faking this whole scene.
I ended up apologizing
For the mistakes I never made.

We promised we'd always stay,
But it's already been a decade
Since we parted ways.
Do you even remember the promises we made?

I think one thing,
And say something else,
When it comes to talking to people.
Sometimes it turns out right,
But most times,
I say what I shouldn't have said.
I overthink it,
And regret it.
So, I stay silent,
Not speaking,
Isolating myself
To avoid hurting others,
Burying my feelings inside,
Even if it's killing me.

If you don't understand
The difference between
Want and Need,
How will you understand
The difference between
Like and Love?

You think you're hiding your lies perfectly clean
But I can sense it the moment you set foot in the room.

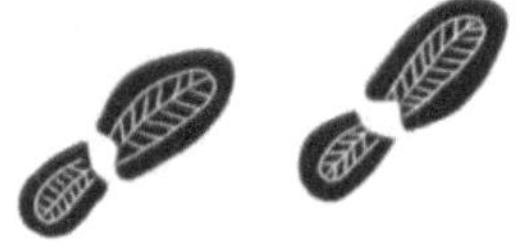

Walking through the streets,
In the middle of the night,
Crying as I walk out of your door,
Saying our last goodbyes.
Walking slowly, thinking you'd call my name,
So I could run back to you.
But you closed the door and never turned back.
I cried out loud, calling out your name.
I didn't know what to do or where to go.
I was staying alive, being dead inside,
Knowing I'm dead and rotting inside your heart.
Somehow, you never returned.
You left me taking the east,
And gave your friends a big feast,
While I took the west,
Trying hard to have a zest.
Hoping we would not cross paths
For the rest of our lives.

I despise you very much,
When I think about all the
Cruel things you've done.
There is a fire raging inside me,
So don't you come near me
Unless you want to
Turn your body into ashes.

There are things I might never say,
Thinking about it would make me cry all-day,
I've been swayed by people's words,
I would never say, but it hurts.
So, I guess I'll stop saying "hello"
If not, it will lead to the drenching of my pillow.

Dear sea,
You're blue and beautiful
And they love you.
I'm blue and betrayed
But they have no clue.

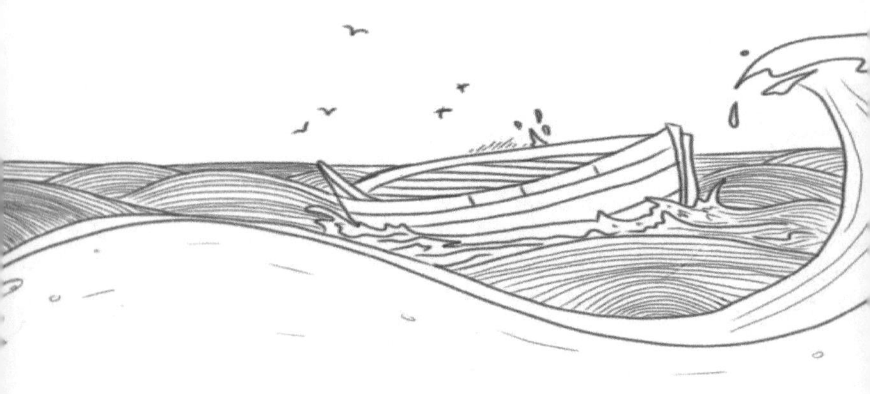

I loved you with
All my heart,
My soul,
My ink and paper,
But you broke my heart
Ripped out my soul,
And crushed my papers
Like it was nothing.

I've been a caged bird,
Trained by people
On what to say and do.
Now that I've been set free,
I'm struggling to fly
In the vastness of the world.

I never wanted the sun to set,
And I never wanted you to leave.
All I wanted to say was, "Stay."
How can I ever let you go
Knowing we'll never meet again?

I've been waiting for you, surreptitiously,
Waiting till the dark,
Hoping for you to arrive.
But you ignored my signs,
Or maybe I was wrong.
Maybe you didn't see them.
I don't know how long I can wait,
But when I leave,
You'll wonder where I went,
And the silence will speak for me.

I thought we were twin flame,
But we burned too red in the end.

I'm tired of telling you
What makes me
Happy,
Sad, and
Angry.
I've explained it a million times,
Yet you still don't understand me.

Not once
You've read me a book,
Written me a letter,
Sung me a song,
Bought me flowers,
Or even held my hand outdoors.
But you claim to be in love with me.
How am I supposed to believe you
When those are the quintessence of love?

I've been chained
By your love,
And been drained
By your talks.

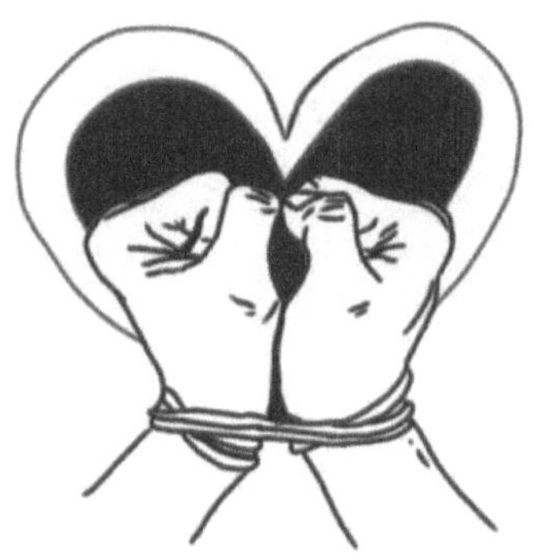

You notice your hair is messier
After the slightest touch of breeze,
You notice the golden sky that gleams right after sunset
And click pictures of them.
You notice the phases of the moon
And admire its beauty all night.
You notice the little coffee stain on your shirt
And strain so much to clean it.
It's wonderful that you're noticing
The little things we forget to notice.
Yet I can't help but notice you
Noticing those things,
But failing to notice me
When I was around you the whole time.

I couldn't deal with my mind
So, if you don't mind,
I'd come over again for you.

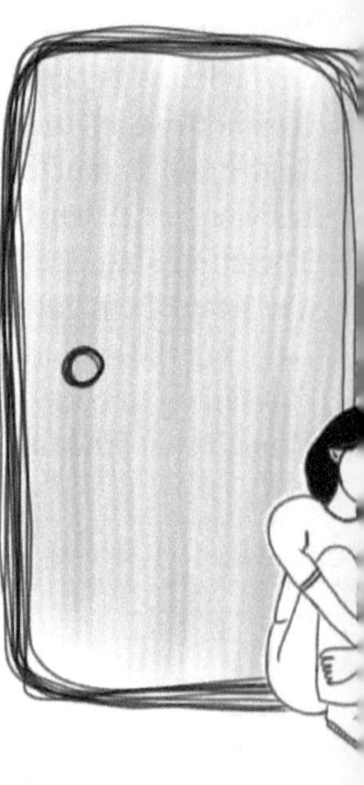

I've been loved thrice
By three different people,
Trying to show me love
In three different ways,
But I never understood them.
Maybe it could be because
I've never really loved myself.

Walking through the town,
Crossing valleys and trees,
Searching for you, my love.
You're not here, you're not there,
You're not anywhere we used to be-
Not in the cabin, nor by the river's side.
Where did you go?

I can hear you in the silence,
I can hear you in the crowds,
Your presence echoes everywhere,
In everything around.
But you've left me feeling unmoored,
Lost in the world you once made whole.

Dear breeze,
Why would no one caress me
Like you do?

You turned me
Into a poet,
And then left me.
What would I write about you now?
The love?
The hurt?
Perhaps I'll write
A book for you-
To show
How I loved you,
How it hurt me,
And how I healed.

I've been stabbed
In my heart
A million times.
It hurt me,
It still aches.
I still have scars.
I will never forget
What they did,
But I forgive them,
As its time for me to heal.

Getting him out of my mind
Was the most difficult part.
Sometimes I think
I'm not over him yet,
But I am over him.
But my heart
Still refuses to believe it.

People say I bring bad luck,
Maybe that's why you left me too.

· · ·

WOMANHOOD

. . .

If she needs to go out,
she can't leave
unless she has:
cooked food,
done the dishes,
cleaned the house,
mopped the floor,
and finished the laundry.

~ Life of a woman after marriage

She always takes care of everyone but herself

~mother

When she confronted those
Who were talking behind her back,
They were terrified of her eyes
Terrified of her next move.
In that moment, they wish they were dead.

~backbiting always puts you in danger

You can go out with your friends.
You can come home at midnight.
You can go wherever you want.
You can do whatever you want.
I'm not going to control you.
I'm never going to demand anything from you.
I'm not going to get angry at you
I'm not even going to ask you anything.

But I think you should at least know this:
I would love it if you'd just
Take me out on a date.
Just us!
Not with family, not with kids.
Just us!

I hope it's not too much to ask,
And I really hope
That someday
You'll find the time to take me out.

~a normal woman's wish

She cries
When she tries to explain things,
When she's angry at someone,
When someone slightly raises their voice,
While watching a sad movie,
While reading a heartbreaking book.

She cries over the little things
Which makes others angry at her.
So, she tries so hard to stop those tears,
But they won't stop rolling down her cheeks.

~ a pure-hearted and sensitive woman

There are some people
Who swear that
They're not racist,
They don't body shame people.
But when it comes to
searching for a bride
For their beloved son,
They become those people
Who find fault in every
Detail of the woman:
The tone of her skin,
The shape of her body,
The texture of her hair,
The colour of her eyes,
The dress she wears,
The way she sits,
The way she stands,
The way she laughs.
I will never understand
The reason behind this process.
They're never going to treat her like a queen.
She's just going to be their unpaid maid.
Then why do they make her
Go through these things?

Stupid rules people follow
When planning for
An arranged marriage.

Rule No. 1
The bride and groom's parents
Should like each other families.

Rule No. 2
The groom's mother
Should like the bride personally,
After asking a ton of questions
About her cooking and cleaning skills.

Rule No. 3
The bride and groom
Must like each other
And agree to their parents' decision.

I know realize the pain my mom endured
Bringing me up these 20 years.
I'm beginning to understand
How tiring it must have been for her
When I wouldn't sleep at night,
When I'd throw tantrums at her,
Especially in my rebellious teens,
When I had those unpredictable mood swings
When I'd been angry at her for no reason,
Yelling at her and breaking things.
How broken must she have been?
How many sleepless nights must she have had?
How many nights she would've cried herself to sleep?
I'm sorry, Mom, for realizing this so late.
But Who would have foreseen
I'd realize this only after becoming a mother?

A woman's life should never
End in her kitchen.

I will raise my daughter
Brave enough to stand up
To the people who hurt her,
Strong enough to speak up
For the truth and the right things,
Kind enough to help the people
Who did and didn't ask for her help.

I used to sleep
For 12 hours straight
Without flinching.
Not even the greatest thunder
Could wake me up.
But now, I wake up 12 times
Just to check on her.
Even the slight sound
Would make me get up.
And that's how motherhood changed me.

Women are always expected
To speak politely and calmly,
Or not speak at all.

~let their voices be heard

Women are
Tender,
Kind,
And caring
In nature.
But they can turn
Fierce,
Brave,
And strong
When it comes
To saving
Their child.
It's in their
Nature, too.

Leaving her home,
Her happiness,
Her 25 years behind,
To begin a completely
New chapter,
By moving into
A stranger's house,
And clueless about
What is going to happen
Is the most dreadful thing
A woman could do.

I used to braid Barbie's hair,
Dress them up in cute clothes,
Have a tea party with my doll friends,
And carry them all day.
At night, I'd keep them close to me,
Covered in princess sheets,
Dreaming about Disney and true love,
Wishing that my dreams would come true.
As a matter of fact, they did!
I French braid my daughter's hair,
Dress her up in beautiful gowns,
Have our tea party with her cute dolls.
At night, she'd sleep with her
Head on my chest, covered in sheets,
Dreaming about love- she became my true love.
Now I'm happy living my inner child's dream.

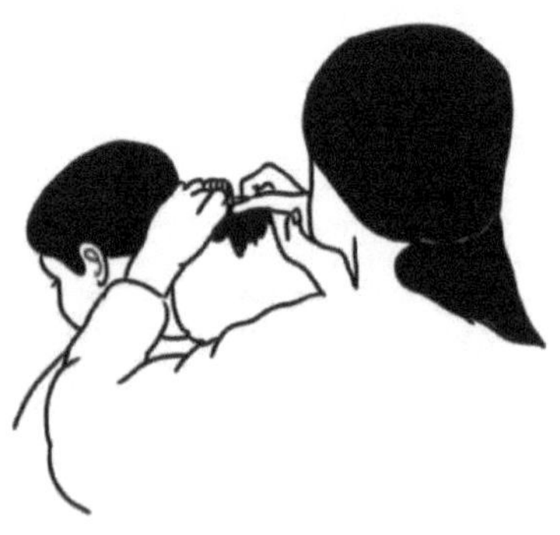

Some parents kill their babies
Because they weren't a son.
Some parents never give their daughters
Their right to education,
Instead, they keep them for doing
The household chores.
Some parents discontinue
Their daughters' education
Once they've attained puberty.
Some parents get their daughters married
Immediately after they've completed their studies.
Then there are those who let their daughters
Go to work and be independent,
But some sickening maniac rapes her, kills her,
And the fear of having a daughter rises.

So, basically, the daughters are killed,
Or forced to work all their childhood,
Or pushed into forceful marriage,
Or raped.

When will this end?
Will this end?

When will they have their right to education?
When will they have a normal childhood?
When will they have the freedom to choose marriage?
When will they have a safe workplace,

And not get raped and killed?
It's so despairing to hear and watch this happen
They are either killed in the beginning
or at the end.

When will this end?
Will this end?

I'll be the greatest warrior,
With the shiniest armour,
Protecting her with my life.
If anyone dares to hurt my queen,
There will be a cut in their heart,
And blood on my sword.

There are some men
Who'd buy flowers
For their woman,
Who'd share the work
When doing household chores,
Who'd listen to their women
When she's upset,
Who'd take care of her
When she's not well,
Who'd take her out
Every once in a while,
Who promised to be with her
Through everything
And are there for her.

~ the kind of man every woman expects

I do not blame all men,
But some need to shut their mouths,
And some need to control their urges.

~mental and physical abuse

To your hard-working hands that work endlessly,
To your cracked feet that keep running tirelessly,
To your eyes that weep for the people who are worthless,
To your heart that keeps breaking numerous times,
And for all the love you gave the world,
They don't deserve you!

When I was a little girl,
I told my mother, "I want to grow like you. "
She said, "You will but enjoy your childhood and create
memories you'd cherish"
I said, "Okay mom," and walked away.

When I was a teen girl,
I told my mother," I wish I was an adult "
She said, "Enjoy your younger self and be carefree, as you
won't get this time back."
I said," Okay mom," and went to depression.

When I was an adult,
I told my mother, "I wish I was still a child"
She said " Darling, never let someone else take your peace
after all you are my little girl and I'll always love you."
I said, "I love you too mom," and cried, hugging her.

Ever since I heard your heartbeat,
My heart started to beat for you.

To My Daughter,

I remember the time
When you'd give me little kicks in my womb,
And now, you're running,
Like you're in a marathon.
I'd do anything to see your cute smiles,
With that little dimple on your face.

I never want you to go through what I did—
I want your childhood to be filled
With memories, joy, and wonder.
I want you to be strong and wise.
I want you to explore everything,
From every tiny insect to every distant land.
I want you to stand up for what's right,
I want you to celebrate your happiness.

Your father and I loved you
From the moment you were within me.
You don't have to be the perfect daughter,
You just have to be you.

I always will shield you
from the horrors of this world,
But I know you'll face them someday.
Remember to be brave, and strong

Because you're special
And you're my daughter.

No matter what,
I'll always love you,
Trust you,
And believe in you.

Love,
Mom♡

To everyone
Who made my mother cry,
One day It'll get back to you
And you'll regret it.

You know you could hire a maid
If you want help with your household work.
That should never be the reason
To search for a bride.

One day her anger and cries
Will burst like a balloon with confetti,
And you'll never grasp the different shades
Of emotions that will rain down.
Yet you'll only blame her
For the outburst that you couldn't predict,
And never ask why it happened,
What pain was buried deep inside,
Or how much she had to blow up
Before she finally burst out.

A Woman always needs three women in her life:

Her mother,
Her sister,
And her best friend.

I survived my childhood
Only because of my sister—
The one who'd rush to me if anything happened,
Who fought the mean girls on my behalf,
And treated me like her own daughter.
Feeding me when I wasn't well,
Consoling me when I cried,
Running to me when I was hurt.
Even when she was starving,
She'd give me the last snack,
Just because I loved it.
She'd let me try on new hair styles,
And paint her face with makeup,
Sharing her favorite toys,
Dancing to our favorite songs,
She'd hold me close during thunderstorms
And when our parents fought.
She'd do anything just to see me smile.
Without her, I am nothing now.

When a person in suit walks down the street,
You show them respect and take a step back.
But when a woman in an abaya passes by,
You see as a threat, and step away in fear.
Yet, those are just clothes,
And they are just human beings.
They feel, just like you do.

A woman is always prettier
When she smiles
And loves herself.

No matter how hard life gets,
You'll always have that one woman,
Who will always love you truly,
Support you through your toughest times,
Guide you through right and wrong,
Never let you down in the eyes of others,
And always be there for you.
Hold onto her tightly
For she is rare.

~that special woman

Being a homemaker
Does not make her dumb.
Her wisdom lies in silence,
In things even you don't know.

When I see my daughter's face,
I see myself as a little girl,
And I remind myself
To be calm, gentle, and kind.
I want to give her a childhood
Free from the fear of hurt or abuse,
By Creating a safe haven for her
Through love, protection, and guidance,
So, she can share everything without fear,
Knowing her mother will always be there for her.

Women should always support other women,
No matter who they are-
A mother, sister, friend
Or even a stranger.
We are intertwined together,
And together we are one.

To the women
Who loved me,
Who helped me,
Who guided me,
Who have always been there for me,
Who encourage me, endlessly-
Without you,
I wouldn't be here.
I owe you everything.

I understand her struggles
Just by looking at her face.
I can see she's not okay
In the way her voice trembles.
I hear her silence,
Even when words are nowhere to be found.

I understand everything
Because I've fought the same battles
With no one by my side.
I know her pain,
Perhaps better than she knows it herself.
And I'd never let her face
Anything alone
Not while I'm here
Were in this fight together.

~fellow women

There's a woman behind
Every woman's success,
A sister, a mother, a friend
Who lifts her up.
But there is also a man behind some women's success
Whose quiet support and love anchor's them,
Making their life sweeter and more supportive.

~to all the silent supporters' brothers, friends, husbands
and, fathers.

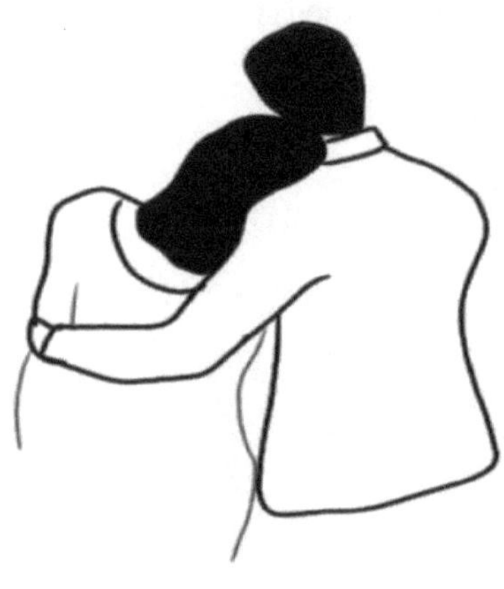

Women supporting women
Create a story most beautifully written.
Each page filled with strength,
Each chapter knitted with love,
Each paragraph blooded by tears.
It's masterpiece only we can write together.

~women supporting other women

Ancestral weight on shoulders
Whispers of fears passed down,
Burdening every woman's heart.
Tales of pain followed,
Unaware of their meaning.

This cycle must break—
Release our child from chains,
From traumas we can't bear.
Let them free from ancestral pain,
And let them write their own tale.

She used to live her life
Sleeping, relaxing,
Taking breaks with no rules.
But now she leaves her whole life behind
And creates and builds a beautiful life,
Just for her children.

She serves them a grand breakfast
And eats the leftovers,
Working tirelessly,
Day after day.
Now she makes rules for herself,
Striving for perfection
Until exhaustion pulls her into sleep.

Oh, woman,
How could you change yourself
So completely?

I've never said "I love you"
To my mother.
The words rise,
But fall back,
Before I could let them out.

She shows her love
In small gestures-
A meal, a touch, a memory held.
I show mine
In calls with no reason,
Just to hear her voice.

We've texted I love you
But never said them out loud
I don't know why-
Maybe fear, habit
Or even tradition.

But I hope that one day,
I'll tell her
How much I love her.

"You are kind,
You are strong,
You are pretty,
You are smart,
You are brave,
You are thoughtful.
Everything happens for a reason.
You'll get over him eventually,
And you are going to be okay.
You will find your soulmate someday.
Until then, I'll always be there for you"
Said the girl, wiping her friend's eyes.

She's the quiet one,
An observer,
She hears murmur in every corner,
Knows everyone who lies and gossips.

She does not like to socialize,
So she fakes her smiles,
Trying to fit in,
Trying to be perfect for everyone.

She always gets lost in her thoughts
Trying to connect every dot.
While others people speak so eloquently,
She talks through her pen and poetry.

As some receive flower bouquets,
She stands in the corner,
Draped in a blue gown,
Waiting for someone to offer her a red rose.

~ an introvert waiting to fall in love

Being born the middle child
Is difficult too;
Nobody listens to you,
Your opinions never matter.
You always get the used things
From your siblings.
And you think you're nobody's favorite.
They call you the crazy one,
But your elder sibling understands you
more than anyone.
They won't say it,
But you're like their child,
Loved with all their heart,
Having faced battles
Far worse than yours.
And would always try to make you happy.

I always wanted to travel beyond the sunset
Yet, I could never set foot from my home past twilight.
The horizon calls me with its light
But my home holds me tight.

...

HEAL

Finally,
The characters
In my head
Are drowning.
I think I've made it.

It's not your fault.
People make mistakes.
You're going to be fine.
You can do this.
You're going to get through this.
You are strong and brave.
You're kind and beautiful.
You deserve all the happiness.
You're not alone.
I'll always be there for you.
I love you.

~ to everyone who is going through a tough time

I'm not going to care anymore
About what others say,
In front of me or behind my back.
I can't deal with those lunatics,
Not anymore.

I am finally in my autumn season
Letting go of my past,
Which I can no longer hold,
And waiting to bloom again-
With colors and flowers
In the season of spring.

Oh, dreamy light,
Subtle and calm,
A sense of serenity.
You have witnessed
The sadness,
The long-distance lovers,
The crying,
The soul seekers,
The dreamers,
The lonely wanderers,
The heartbreak.
You have known everything,
Yet you somehow comfort people
By singing a silent lullaby
Along with the winds,
Bringing calmness and peace.

~the moon

No one can rescue you
From your drowning thoughts.
Only you can save yourself.

~self help

Dear sun,
Thank you for shining every day,
Making me smile,
Giving me hope,
To have a better day.

People may think I've changed.
Yes, I have.
This is the real me.
I used to hide behind a mask
To spare your feelings.
But you forced me to change
So, I did.
And now,
This is the real me.

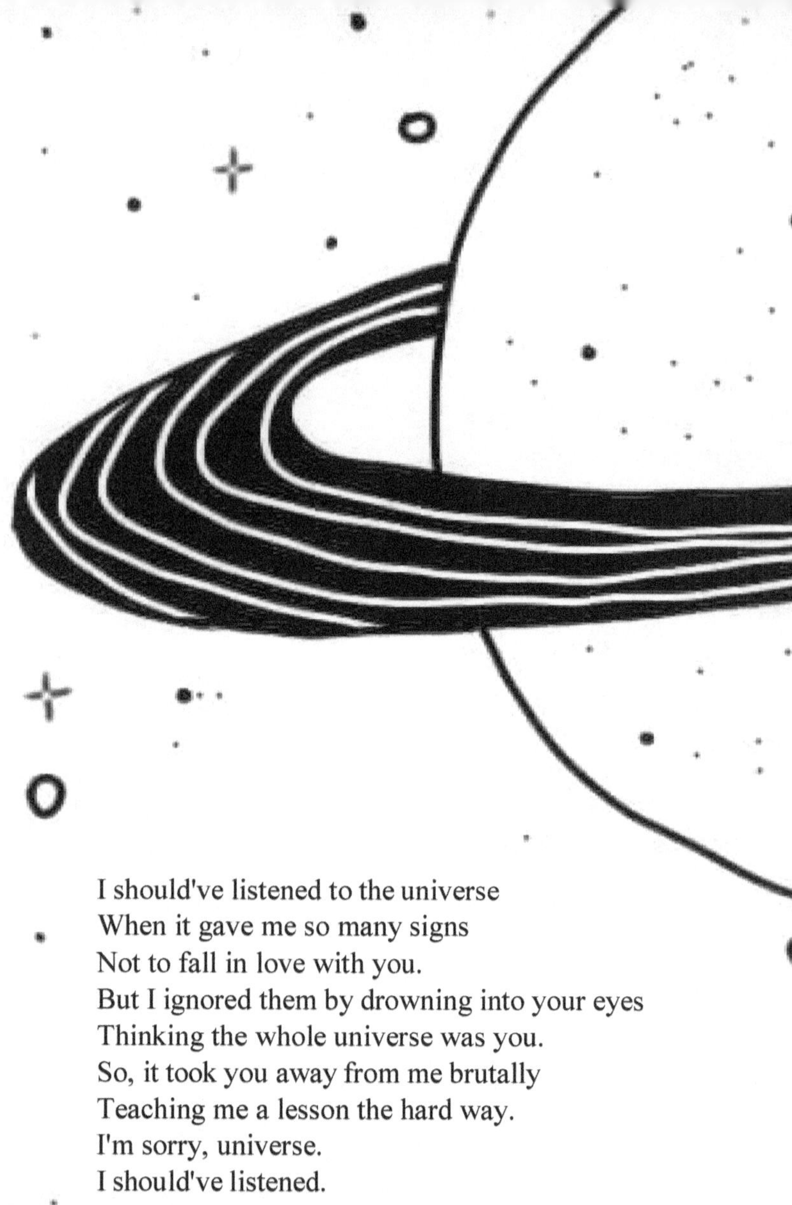

I should've listened to the universe
When it gave me so many signs
Not to fall in love with you.
But I ignored them by drowning into your eyes
Thinking the whole universe was you.
So, it took you away from me brutally
Teaching me a lesson the hard way.
I'm sorry, universe.
I should've listened.

~ the realization

Sometimes, I wish
I could go back to the days
When we were in love.
But then I remember
How it ended.
So I ditch that thought
And get back to work.

After seeing the beaming sunlight,
It feels like I've been underwater
For a long time.

~ recovering from trauma

This world is no fairytale,
And bad people can't be destroyed.
Evil witches linger around us,
Shape shifting, casting spells,
Plotting to destroy us in every way.
Being soft and kind,
Like a princess, won't work here.
Be brave-
Like a warrior on the battlefield.

Sometimes, I just want to sit on the beach
And lose myself in the music of waves.

You don't have to live for other people
Or the opinions they hold of you.
They're always going to talk
They're always hurt you,
Leaving you feeling utterly alone.
So start living your life
On your own terms,
For you,
And only you.

I have survived
Many thunderstorms
Since you left.
Getting past you
Wasn't so hard after all.

But the best teachers
I've ever had
Were the people around me-
Who taught me about love and hurt,
And the nature surrounding me,
Which taught me how to heal.

You look good in the mirror,
But the camera tells another tale.
People's views may differ too,
Yet that won't change what you know.
You're being beautiful in every way
And you don't need to hear it from them.

When I'm feeling blue,
I run to see the blue sky.
It heals me,
Turning my imagination real
Through the passing of clouds.

When I'm in a dark place
I run to see the dark sky.
It heals me,
As twinkling stars
And the silver moon
Invite me into their family,
Reminding me I'm never alone.

You're exactly where you're supposed to be.
Trust the process and have faith.

I'm not going to force you.
I'm not going to beg you.
I'm not going to chase you.
Those days are long gone.

I've been Sitting at the beach at the golden hour
Watching the ebb and flow of waves,
Listening to the birds and the breeze.
As I think about finding peace
The warm wind softly caresses my hair,
Urging me to let go of things hard to bear.

But it has never been plain sailing.
There are still creatures fighting in my head,
Like the sea creatures swimming on the bed
I want to wipe out the things on my mind
Just as the sea wipes out my writing from the sand
It seems I'm dark and blue just like the deep blue sea.

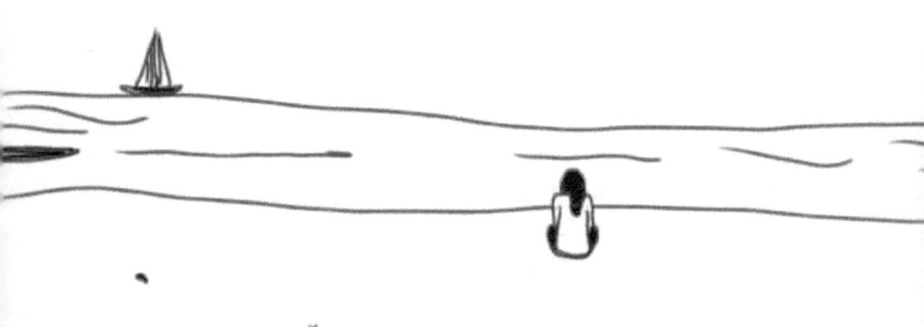

To see the golden sunset
After a terrible day
Is what brings me peace.

The constant chatter in my mind
Disappears when you are with me.

I always chose others before choosing myself.
But I've learned my lesson now.
This time, I'll choose me
Before anyone else.

My mind was already a mess,
And the people within made it worse.
I tried so hard to clean up,
To make them leave,
But it never worked.
So I took them trekking,
Led them to a cliff,
And pushed them off,
Hoping for a little peace.

~healing

Taking your life is not the solution
To the most heartbreaking situation
You've ever faced in your life.
It should always be the desire to live
To prove and to show them
That you're braver and stronger.

~ stay strong

The universe always whispers its signs
Yet we could never listen,
With the chaos in our head.
But if we pause and take a deep breath,
We could finally hear
The universe guiding us to the right path.

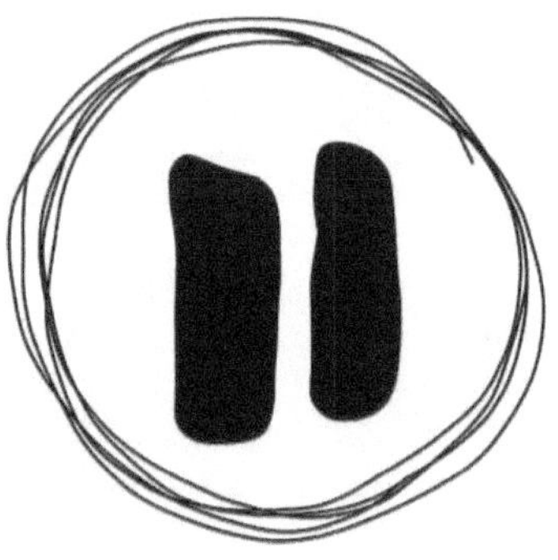

your
inner
child
does
not
need
other's
love;
it
needs
to
be
loved
by
you

In the end,
I always
Want to go home
And sleep in my bed.

~ comfort

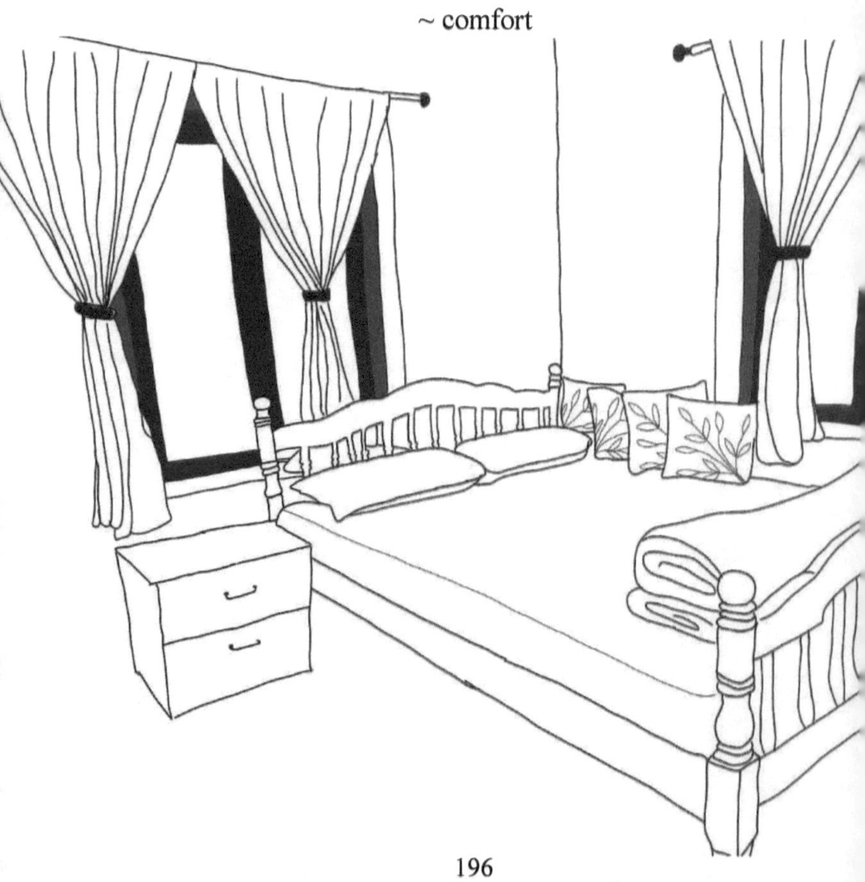

If thinking of it
Makes your eyes red
And your heart bleed-

                       Let it go.

It's not worth the pain.

A hidden suitcase under my bed,
I pulled it out, dusted it off.
Once, the things inside belonged solely to me,
But now, it seems, they belong to spiders too.
I opened it, and found my wooden jewelry box,
Lifted the lid, and old memories hit me,
Familiar yet distant.
A broken, silent watch,
And a color faded ring.
I thought these would bring me sorrow
So I hid them away.
But now that I see them,
They carry only soft, worn-out happy memories.
A little old,
A little faded.

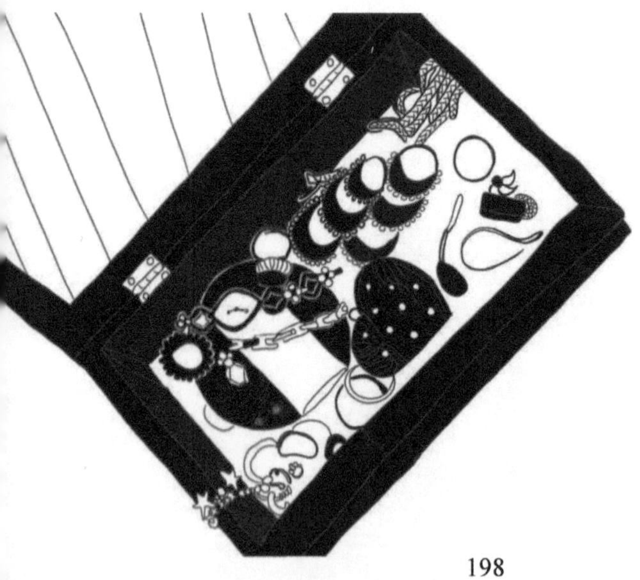

While some people try to conquer the world,
There are others who choose delusion instead
X Dreading the outside, knowing its cruelty.
Where people act like high school teens
Lying, cheating, stirring up drama.
They'd rather disappear forever,
Live quietly in their fantasies,
Far away from a world that's harsh and mean.

The moon and the flowers debated,
Each claiming their beauty was the best rated.

The moon said,
"I light the world through the darkest night
 Bringing calmness to others' lives "

The flowers replied,
"We color the earth with our beauty
 And spread the world with our fragrance"

They asked the mountain,
Sturdy with wisdom,
To settle their debate once and for all.

The mountain said,
"Both of you have admirers,
But you are perfect together-
Moonlit flowers, a peaceful night."

While people survive the wild
With hatred and thorns,
You're surviving the wild
With kindness and flowers.
You're not like the others-
You are a wallflower in the wild.

Some days, you're broken,
Utterly sad and lonely.

Some days, you're happy,
Loved and laughing.

Nothing is going to last.
Things always change.

Tenderness fills my heart,
I could so easily fall apart.
Give me reasons to feel alive,
Help my grieving soul revive.

Sadness shadows my life,
I give up after every strife.
Give me reasons to stay with you,
Help me mend our love anew.

But happiness has finally returned,
When I left you, my lesson learned.
No more reasons needed to be okay
I'll never ask for your help again.

You can't make a dead flower bloom,
Nor can you make him love you again.
It's long gone, withered, and dead.

~some things are meant to end.

Your first priority must be-
Sleep
And health-
Before anything else.

~self-care

She always searches for
The angels inside others,
Bringing out their good side.
But she must realize-
Sometimes, demons lurk
Behind those sweet eyes.
And she could never bring
Out the bright beam inside them.
No matter how hard she tries
She will only get trapped,
Inside their dark room.

I do not belong in a wolf pack,
I prefer being the lone wolf.
I do not belong in the city,
I'd rather roam the countryside.
I do not seek the bright morning light,
I find peace in a darkened room,
Standing by the window,
Watching the stars.

Trespassers pluck and stomp you down,
Yet flowers bloom in the scars they left behind.
You're slowly healing, and one day you'll see-
You've grown into a beautiful garden,
This time, you stand strong,
And put up your "No Trespassing" sign.

www.ingramcontent.com/pod-product-compliance
Lightning Source LLC
Chambersburg PA
CBHW031124130726
47988CB00006B/2207